the death of
al-Hallaj

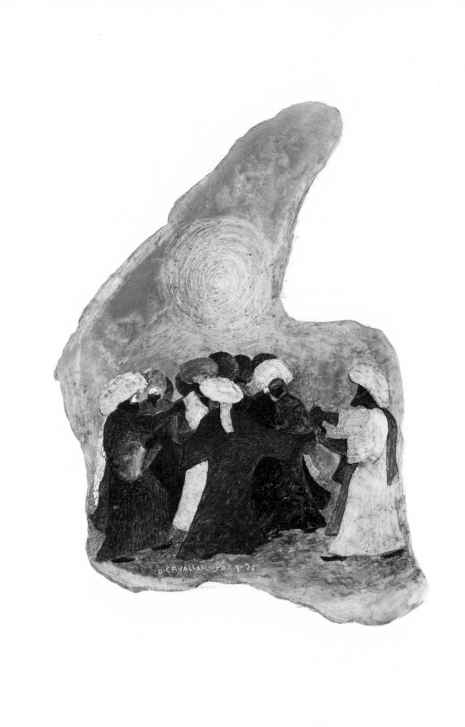

the death of al-Hallaj

A Dramatic Narrative

by Herbert Mason

UNIVERSITY OF NOTRE DAME PRESS

NOTRE DAME   LONDON

An earlier version of *The Death of al-Hallaj* was published
as a special supplement of *The American Poetry Review,*
July–August 1974.

9 8 7 6 5 4 3 2

Library of Congress Cataloging in Publication Data

Mason, Herbert, 1932–
    The death of al-Hallaj.

    1. al-Ḥallāj, al-Ḥusayn ibn Mansūr, 858 or 9–922—
Drama. I. Title.
PS3563.A7923D4   813'.5'4   79-4403
ISBN 0-268-00842-6
ISBN 0-268-00843-4 pbk.

Manufactured in the United States of America

For Albert Duclos

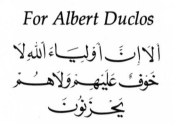

أَلَا إِنَّ أَوْلِيَاءَ اللهِ لَا
خَوْفٌ عَلَيْهِمْ وَلَاهُمْ
يَحْزَنُونَ

Preface

The Death of al-Hallaj is a recital of the
thought and spiritual way of a tenth-century Muslim
mystic who was executed in Baghdad for heresy in
309 of the Hijra, A.D. 922. Husayn ibn Mansur,
known as *hallāj al-asrār* ("the carder of consciences"
or "the reader of hearts"), his disciple Ibn Ata, and
protectress Shaghab (the Caliph's mother), and his
antagonist Ibn Dawud are presented in silhouette
form against the background of a narrative account
transmitted by his son Hamd. The form of presenta-
tion is that of the *samāᶜ* or "hearing" of a spiritual
teacher's words on God, life, and the world. The
mixing of anecdote, account, poetry, prayer, and
exhortation was a familiar practice in medieval Islam
both in literature and in study sessions of experts on
the sources and branches of sacred law, mysticism,
grammar, belles lettres, or traditions concerning the
Prophet. The higher purpose of the *samāᶜ* was to
stimulate recollectedness and a deeper orientation to

the will of God. *The Death of al-Hallaj*, therefore, is a celebration of a character and his vision, not a play. The action is implicit, not explicit.

In the "recital" Hallaj at times practices *shath*, or conversation with God. It is part of his imprudent character that he does not keep this conversation to himself. Religiously Hallaj may remind one at moments of Hasidic Jewish mystics, at others of a combination of St. John of the Cross and St. Francis, of St. Joan, or of Jesus, by inner devotion and by what we imagine they may have said to friends and to God on unrecorded occasions. He is beyond fear and therefore strange and frightening. He is a lover of God and of humanity who simply cannot measure out his love in moderation. He is imprisoned but free.

It is helpful to remember that the century of Hallaj's birth (in A.D. 858) was a century of great intellectual ferment and scientific experimentation in the Islamic world. The Greek sciences and philosophies had recently become part of the Muslim consciousness. The new analytical method led to technological advances as well as to heretofore inconceivable theological speculations and liberties. Astronomy, mathematics, physiology, botany, to say nothing of alchemy, were growing preoccupations of the age. Natural scientists even developed the idea, though they lacked the technology, for the construction of a robot possessing only the ideal qualities and virtues of a man. Religious leaders haggled over theological fine points of Qur'anic exegesis and sacred law. Each professional group and religious sect was in the process of defining its distinguishing features and of developing its own highly specialized and technical language. It was an age of experts and of pedantry.

It was also an age of abundance and opulence, of obsession with physical beauty, both male and female, of music, dance, eating, imbibing, of luxuriating in expensive imported materials, fashions, silks and perfumes. As one might expect, it was simultaneously an age of economic and racial inequity and injustice. In the case of the many black slaves and poor bedouins this took the form of outright misery and starvation. Corruption and waste in government, private misuse of public treasure and trust, the personal ambitions and greeds of caliphs, vizirs, judges, jurists, theologians, extremist sects, and praetorian guards were among the causes. The intelligentsia, including poets, scholars, and belle-trists, dreaded the provinces, so that Baghdad was swollen with more or less sophisticated people scrambling for positions and purses offered or with-held by bored, self-serving patrons. Put simply, it was an age of inflation, both in living and in rhetoric; of instant violence and of constant vying for power at various levels of institutional authority.

Hallaj, knowledgeable in law, religious tradi-tion, and letters, had, like other mystical thinkers of his time, developed a technical lexicon, even as he preached against esotericism and excessive spe-cialism or legalism in the practice of religion. From his modest Persian origins in southwestern Iran, he came to enjoy the patronage of the rich and power-ful of Baghdad, most notably that of the Caliph's own mother, even as he preached publicly against the Caliph's corrupt practices. He wrote both trans-parently simple spontaneous verses of the intimacy of God's love and abstruse theological tracts. Above all he immersed himself totally in the spirit of God through love. The keynotes of his way were friendship and fidelity to the very end, and the belief that it was the Friend who had found and befriended him, not the reverse.

In one of his odes, he wrote

The sum of everything I am
You are. And everything I am
Is Mystery. I have confused You
With my little meaning.

It is You I've been in love with
And been crushed, in moments
When You let Yourself
Become my prisoner.

I mourn in being exiled
From my home—I chose it so;
My enemies are happy
In my sorrow.

* * * * * * * *

O my request and hope,
My home, my very breath,

My faith,
My worldly fate,

Say to me 'I have rescued you.'
O my hearing and my sight,
Why do You keep me still
At such a distance?

Though You are hidden
To my eyes,
My heart perceives You
In the distance.[1]

He was punished, many of his contemporary and later mystics believed, because of such confusion of himself with God and because he refused to keep God's secret gifts private to himself, as they insisted was the sign of their vocation. He saw both objections as misunderstandings of love.

In another ode, he wrote

---

1. My translations from Arabic. The first and third odes quoted here were published in full in *Introduction to Arabic Literature*, ed. I. Lichtenstadter (Boston: Twayne, 1974). Used with permission of G. K. Hall & Co.

In my inmost heart there is a pearl
I cannot touch.

I tremble when my thievish doubts
Draw near.

It is a gift my love has given me
To keep in trust.

Though blind, by it I see;
Naive, I am made wise.

The Seven Sleepers know this love.
They are my friends.

Time stops in the shadow
Of their mountain.

In its hush my love returns
To claim His pearl.

What was most surprising to his contem-
poraries, but not to some of his disciples, and what
has helped keep his memory alive in the Muslim
world and drawn comparison to Jesus from other

quarters is that, from all accounts, he accepted the judgment as just and welcomed the martyrdom without any bitterness. A typical saying of his is, "When God takes a heart, He empties it of all that is not Himself; when He loves a servant of His, He incites others to persecute him, so that His servant will come to draw himself more closely to Him." "Hell is nothing," he once said, "compared to the cost of my emptiness when You have left me." God's lovers, he believed, were total witnesses, not onlookers, to love.

He was resigned to death but believed profoundly in renewal and resurrection. In another ode, he wrote

> Murder me now, my faithful friends,
> For in my murder is my life.
>
> My death would be to go on living
> And my life would be to die.
>
> To me removal of my self
> Would be the noblest gift to give

And my survival in my flesh
The ugliest offence, because

My life has tired out my soul
Among its fading artifacts.

So kill me, set aflame
My dried out bones

And when you pass by my remains
In their deserted grave,

You will perceive the secret of my Friend
In the inmost folds of what survives.

One moment I'm a sheikh
Who holds the highest rank,

And then I am a little child
Dependent on a nurse

Or sleeping in a box
Within the brackish earth.

My mother gave her father birth,
Which was a marvel I perceived,

And my own daughters whom I made
Became my sisters in this way to me,

Not in the world of time
Nor through adulteries.

So gather all the parts together
Of the glowing forms

Of air and fire
And pure water

And sow them in unwatered soil;
Then water it from cups

Of serving maids
And flowing rivulets;

And then, when seven days have passed,
A perfect plant will grow.

    In an age whose preponderant fashions were
self-indulgence, artificiality, cleverness and criticism
rather than creativity, an age of imitation of "the

Greek philosophers" and manifold decadence, it was left to the mystics to be commonsensical, intuitive, spontaneous, simple, profound. But there was much excess as a result. Over the strong objection of his early teachers, Hallaj, three times the faithful pilgrim to Mecca, increasingly released himself to the madness of his own spiritual inspiration and inner sense of truthfulness. He danced as an alternative to abstractionism and despair. For all the learning gained by his century, there had been much drying up of the primitive and fresh springs of Islamic inspiration. He believed in this direct inspiration from the Source in a time when religious officials, like others, had become excessively prudent and dissimulative or had even lost the sense of what their origin and callings were. He emphasized the brotherhood of faith, which is how he believed Muhammad's community had first been conceived. He saw himself, not as a crypto-Christian—which his martyrdom suggests and which his enemies accused him of being—but as a renewer and mystical complementer, even fulfiller, of Muhammad's early vocation.

xvii

Our knowledge of him is due largely to the devotion and scholarship of the late Professeur Louis Massignon of the Collège de France. In 1907, during an expedition to Mesopotamia, Massignon, then a young archaeologist and linguist, was mistaken by Turkish officials as a French spy and was imprisoned. In ailing health, he was released into the care of a prominent Baghdadi family, who during his convalescence shared with him their knowledge of the biography and poetry of Hallaj. By an extraordinary affinity and sensitivity Massignon, a Christian, was able to cross over into the historical, linguistic, religious, and cultural consciousness of the other. He entered a profound friendship and came to share the spiritual fidelity of the Muslim whose "passion"[2] he was to transmit in a series of major studies, editions,

---

2. My four-volume edition and translation with biographical introduction of Louis Massignon's *La Passion d'al-Hallaj* will appear in the Bollingen Series, Princeton University Press, 1980. A complete updated bibliography on Hallaj is included in vol. 4.

and translations. Especially important, he became
something of an itinerant scholar like Hallaj himself,
traveling to places Hallaj had been known to travel,
throughout the Middle East, Iran, Khurasan, and
Western India, collecting any and every work by him
and memorial to him that had survived the cen-
turies. Massignon discovered that Hallaj was indeed
very much alive, often in folkloric ways, in the popu-
lar imagination and in circles of religious orders in
remote areas of the Islamic world. In recent decades
Hallaj has been the subject of a number of plays
and poems by leading Arab, Persian, and
Turkish writers.

Massignon himself always felt that he had
been discovered and plumbed by Hallaj and that
their linking was not a matter of investigative re-
search or transcultural curiosity, but was a friendship, a love, a rescue. Clearly the Hallajian way im-
plies a certain surrender of self, an expatriation of
mind, an absorption with the life and spirit of another than oneself. Friendship and fidelity are its
keynotes and infectiously become those of others
who come to know him.

The Death of al-Hallaj
was first presented in a concert reading at Harvard's
World Religion Center on February 27, 1974,
with the author, Albert Duclos, James Malcolm,
and Annemarie Schimmel in the
principal roles.

Characters in order of appearance:

HAMD, Hallaj's son, the narrator

IBN DAWUD, Jurist

IBN ATA, Hallaj's friend and disciple

HALLAJ

SHAGHAB, Caliph Muqtadir's mother,
a supporter of Hallaj

Part One

1

HAMD NARRATING

My father stared at the walls of the city,
Said to his guards, who didn't hear his words,
Who had been warned not to listen to his words
Lest they be seduced by them to set him free:
There is a time we must return from where
We've been, carrying the journey inside
To rebuild what others have torn down,
Or to destroy old temples in ourselves . . .
To annihilate the temple. The guards closed their ears.
He was led into Baghdad on a mule
Drawn by a guard and ringed by soldiers
To keep the crowd from hurting him,
For the orders were to bring him safely in.
The general Mu'nis had ordered a placard
Tied around his neck which read "An Agent
Of the Carmathians." These were the most feared

3

And despised people of the day, because
Their agents spread ideas in secret
Among the poor and blacks which led
To riots in the streets against the Caliph
And the law. And Hamid, the old corrupt
Tax-farmer, Mu'nis' friend, may God protect
Us from his kind, wanted to become vizir
And knew the only way was to smear our great
Vizir Ibn Isa, may God hold him close to Him
For his goodness to all men, who was my father's friend
And who had also been lenient toward
Carmathians. To link my father
And Carmathians in the public's and the Caliph's mind
And then present himself as the stronger and more loyal
Defender of law and order—this was Hamid's plan,
And this explains the ferocity with which
He tracked my father down:
Not heresy, but greed. Scribes came each day
To Hamid's house with pamphlets forged
In my father's hand. A letter to a friend
Was the one they fastened on, in which he
Called for "the destruction of the temple."

4

They said he meant to pillage Mecca, the way
Carmathians later did. His disciple, Ibn Ata,
Said he meant "the temple of one's self."
The words he heard from him in prison, and
Which I only partly understand, were
Carefully recorded and concealed until
It was safe, after the death of Hamid.

2

HAMD NARRATING

The one who brought about my father's death,
Who stood in opposition to his thought
And framed the legal arguments against
His teaching and his person, was noted
As a scholar of the law and as a
Poet of aesthetic love: Ibn Dawud.
Ibn Ata tried hard to change his mind,

5

To show him through sincerity the truth
His master taught, thinking sincerity
And the support of lofty friends sufficed.

      *   *   *

IBN ATA

Our beloved Vizir Ibn Isa and
Shaghab the Caliph's mother are still his
Followers . . . . And his testament of faith
Is sound . . . . He has not preached sedition.

IBN DAWUD

And yet his words suggest, you must admit,
That God sees many ways, not one true way,
To lead a Muslim life; and there are hints
In his obsession with fire and light
That he is still attached to the old ways
Of his grandfather, a Zoroastrian.
Couple that with the evidence of magic,
The bringing back to life of the heir apparent's

6

Parrot and the staunching of the Caliph's
Diarrhea, to say nothing of the woman's oath
That he seduced her daughter entrusted
To his spiritual care. It is not
The usual soundness. Oh I admit
He has enjoyed support in high places, but you
Must realize Hamid is Vizir now.
The old support your master had is gone.
Power is not held by the same hands long;
I'm sure your master's wisdom teaches that.
Now he is vulnerable like all men.

IBN ATA

So you imagine he is yours at last.
You believe you have won.

IBN DAWUD

Mine? I have no personal desire to
See him beaten. He is a menace, a threat
To order. He is the age's symbol of

Confusion. And if I can allow myself
One craving it is for order and a
Restoration of our faith in law.

IBN ATA

But I and others know he is its true
Restorer, not its enemy. There are many
In high places eager to condemn him
Because he speaks the truth about them. We all
Know how the Caliph lives: the speculation
He allows the bankers like Hamid, the way
He spends the money from the Public Chest
On banquets for his friends, and the lavish gardens he con-
        structs
With exotic shrubbery and lush foreign flowers,
When there are people rioting for bread.

IBN DAWUD

I have always admired the Caliph's taste
For flowers.

8

IBN ATA

You really are supremely insincere.

IBN DAWUD

"Supremely" is a word I'm loath to use,
And "insincere," if you mean the opposite
Of what led Hallaj to excess,
Yes, I am, though I prefer the word "cautious"
For those who still appreciate the law
And never break it. "Sincerity" or "insincerity"
Are sentiments, not laws. They stand
Outside our competence to judge. Do I detect
In you a secret divination of this man?
You make him out a victim of the law.
He cannot be a victim, as the law is just,
But a threat to public order.

IBN ATA

I will not give my signature for your
Consensus. He is innocent of what

9

You charge him with. And do not count on the
Caliph's mother doing nothing. She's still
His friend and powerful at court.

IBN DAWUD

Yes. She will try to help, but she was raised
In the palace and thus is well-prepared
To recognize when fate has turned against her.
It is too bad that Hallaj is a creature of excess,
For him, for her, for everyone. I am trying
To warn you for your own good, not for mine:
He did not understand that even God loves to excess some-
     times
And burns His lovers out, then discards them.
Your Hallaj was a good scholar and a good poet
Who simply was too much in love—with love.

IBN ATA

You sounded almost sentimental then.

10

IBN DAWUD

No, but sentiment has its place
In the overall proportioning of things.

IBN ATA

Of course, you might have been her favorite
If not for Hallaj.

IBN DAWUD

If she admires him to such excess
Then I can do without her admiration.

IBN ATA

Of course you can.

11

HAMD NARRATING

When Ibn Ata visited the prison,
He found my father talking to Allāh.

*   *   *

HALLAJ

I'm close to everyone I know, in love
Perhaps? Is there danger in that, O Lord?
There is from one who's jealous of our love,
Who wants to draw us from all those we love,
To separate us from the ones we touch,
But You are kind. You leave us with our needs,
Not with our sense of glory. You never
Raise us high above the ones we love, that
Is *Your* compassion. Only the gibbet

12

Raises us, the hatred of the jealous one.
I love to touch. I fall in love often.
It is easy. Men and women, children,
Strangers on a journey whom I do not touch
Out of respect but yearn to in their strange
Warmths and difference. I ache
To love, to touch, and not to hide in love.
Keep me from ever becoming
Too old to love *You*, Lord.
But age me quickly in bitterness
Coldness jealousy cruelty.
You are my model:
You are not afraid to love a creature
Ugly as myself.

     IBN ATA

Have I interrupted you?

     HALLAJ

No, a friend can never interrupt.

13

IBN ATA

I brought you candied dates, the kind you like.

(HALLAJ *takes the dates and, sitting on the bench beside his friend, begins to eat.*)

IBN ATA

Have you everything you need in here?

HALLAJ

Once I would have answered "yes"
Like an earnest martyr who wants to show
He lives on little. But now, at my age,
I can live without essentials but
Not luxuries, one of
Which is having friends who bring me candy.

IBN ATA

I never can get used to the idea
Of your captivity in here.

14

HALLAJ

Yes, there is a difference, isn't there,
Between *captivity* and being captive *here*.

IBN ATA

Please don't make plays on words with me.
The time's too serious for that.

HALLAJ

I'm sorry, my friend, a harmless mischief.

IBN ATA

Would you have me believe you're what they claim—
Mischievous?

HALLAJ

I am.
But I don't hatch plots as they do.

15

I enjoy disguises. Not high mischief, just low,
A kind of entertainment for myself
When I have nothing else to do.

IBN ATA

You must know they have called you mad.

HALLAJ

Yes, they have called me mad.
They have called me everything.
But I am not everything.
I may be mad. When I am spoken to
By the One Who speaks to me in crowds
Or in the midst of conversation
On another subject, when suddenly He speaks,
I open my mouth and out come His words.
They look at me and think I never listen
Or am constantly distracted,
Addicted to nonsequiturs.
In short, mad,

16

Deranged, old age losing its mind.
I *am* losing my mind, that part of it
That thinks it can divorce the heart at will
As in a temporary marriage, a brief
Experiment in love. Love is total,
My friend, carrying us forever
Where it goes. It is not experimental
And it knows no term. Even one
Who turns from love in bitterness
Has failure to remind him of its loss,
And longing. Bitterness is love's decrepitude,
The saddest of all states. For of all our failures
The failure to love is the only one
Not curable.
The failure to achieve when yearning to
Has always convalescence for its cure;
But ceasing to desire, that is fatal.
Only desire sees me through this work of
Dying, the thought that impassioned love
Can overcome the cold gods.
Have I said something strange,
Do you think I'm really mad?

17

IBN ATA

They also claim that you're unqualified
To judge the things you say and teach to men.

HALLAJ

Oh, that is far more serious than mad: *unqualified!*
My enemies are right. I always learn more from them
Than friends. They see me clearly as I am.

(Ponders.)

That is another thing unique in God:
He sees like an enemy but is a friend.
I take His judgments very seriously.
God says, you are not qualified, Hallaj,
But go ahead and say it anyway,
Everywhere. I protest, but don't You know
The audience consists of brilliant orators
And sages, of experts without peer,
To speak to them is very bold or lunatic,
My Lord. And then it crosses my mind,

18

Our God is amused at my absurdities.
He too must have capacity for laughter
If he has been the author of my foolishness.
Unless He doesn't know. And every expert
On religion knows that's inconceivable.
So, I conclude at least I'm pleasing to my Lord.
But let's suspend judgment of God for awhile.
You're dealing with a perfect fool, my friend.
I hope I teach you something, but I don't know what.
I am afraid you will not find wisdom here.

(Touches head.)

IBN ATA

Why do you mock your own wisdom?

HALLAJ

At sixty-four my gray hairs hide
Massive stupidity. I possess neither
Beauty nor light, but desire both.

19

You can see how flattering it was
Of that woman to suggest
Her daughter could be attracted—

IBN ATA

No, she said you tried to seduce the girl.

HALLAJ

Did I? *(pauses)*
I guess I am a leerer at the young—
Aren't we all these days,
With all the lovely men and women on display,
Performers, acrobats, and models, who parade
About with their physical opulence
That the angels envied of Adam
And bowed down before, without God's asking—
All but that mad ascetic, Satan,
Who couldn't bear beauty being fleshed,
Visible tangible sensual real.
His Hell is simply living with desire

20

In a universe where God is desireless
And nothing is touched or touching.
Cold, too cold for me.

IBN ATA

How can you talk about such things?
You're playing right into your enemies' hands.

HALLAJ

I can talk about such things
Because I am accusable of being
Old and dirty, a worthless
Old fool, God's throwaway, perhaps. Because
I would never have wanted to grow wise
Among the wise, or old among the old. I am not up
To such *success*. I want to be eternally young
In Him, eternally filled with desire,
For He is the Essential Desire.
I am willing to be accused, hung up
For all to see, to have light squeezed

21

From my ageing darkness, by God;
His spark, eternal for me,
May it flash in my heart
And I be His darkness.

IBN ATA

You *are* imprudent, just as they say.

HALLAJ

Oh yes. Yes. I am a failure in that virtue.

IBN ATA

But what you have done is something else.
It is something more important, much more.
You showed them that religion is concern
For justice—truth—for all humanity.
You showed them that our God is not a book
To read and close at will, not a subject
For the exegetes and jurisconsults

22

To read exclusively for laws
That can replace the sacred
In the people's hearts—God's presence here
Among us—with solemn prudences
And formal obligations.

HALLAJ

I am impressed at what this person did
Whom you describe. Surely the world has changed.
Surely we are saved. Oh praise be to God.

(Skips for joy.)

The Day of Resurrection is at hand.
Alas, we still begin again in a
World too like the others we have known.
You are still too ambitious for your friend.
I've shown them nothing, effected less than
Little by this life of mine that is
Peculiar to myself. Are you shocked?
Or disappointed? Both are in your face.

23

Religion is not anyone's *concern*, but His.
It is God's gift of Himself to things
He brings to life with His desire.

IBN ATA

Then what *is* the meaning of your teaching,
Of your imprisonment, of your life?

HALLAJ

I have the feeling I shall spend my days
Of confinement being asked the meaning
Of the meaning of the meaning until
My soul and meanings are exhausted by
Analyses. I'm sorry, I did not mean
To hurt you, dear friend. Your face betrays
My selfishness. The meaning is, we are two parrots.
One is imprisoned here so the other may be free
To sing His words. We must be substitutes for each.
It is His desire.

24

(A pause between them. They muse apart.)

IBN ATA

(after a long silence)

Who is He?

HALLAJ

He is His lettered sign to us. H–u–W–a.
His essence is separate from His letters.

IBN ATA

How can we enter Him if He is separate?

HALLAJ

By removing ourself as vowels from His signs
And letting Him be vowels in us. He then enters

25

The signs with His transforming union. And then
Utters Himself clearly in the only true eloquence.
His Oneness is His wisdom.

IBN ATA

Are you also a grammarian?

HALLAJ

I am only His parrot in a cage.

IBN ATA

Is the world then a prison? Are you saying that?

HALLAJ

The world is not something other
Than ourselves and Him.
If I may depart from character,
I think you are really asking

26

If religion can be action
For improving it. I know that you
Are anxious for more action.

IBN ATA

But you yourself took action
When you marched with the Zanj
Against the war,
When you spoke out for the blacks,
When you preached against the Caliph's
And his bankers' speculating on
Their hidden stores of gold and wheat.

HALLAJ

But that is not religion in itself.
We must not think that speaking out
Can be a substitute for meditation of Allāh.
A breed of empty heroes will emerge,
For all it takes is momentary courage
And the crowd does all the rest. No,

27

It is harder to contemplate our God
Than to utter a few words on His behalf.
But sometimes we are called to be a mouthpiece
For the inarticulate, maybe to lose our lives.
But even dying on the gibbet is nothing
More than one rung on the ladder,
Not the last. . . . The last is His alone
Where He embraces us. For then we know
Our heart and mind are one like His
Without this separation anymore. I am not a
Theologian, as you can see; only a prisoner
Pulled to the Center . . . the theologian, that is,
Who separates the heart and mind, like Satan,
Who was so conditioned in his love he couldn't bear
God's giving unity to man. He always tried
To make God's unity seem inaccessible.
I am worried about those who concentrate
Too much on fine distinctions, as in the case of faith,
Instead of witnessing His nearness.
But I understand, for we are all closer
To Satan's love than to our God's.

28

IBN ATA

There are so many things I want to ask. . . .
But you speak quickly and I think slowly.
Can I ask you one at a time?
You speak of Satan . . . and his fall through love
I do not understand, and isn't it forbidden
To speak of this?

HALLAJ

Then how can you understand
If it's forbidden to speak of this? Satan is
A nature preceding and kindred to our own.
He has the jealousy of all those who precede;
The conviction that his way of working things
Is best—and the fear
That his creator has fallen out of love.
Hence, he accuses God of madness in creating man
And then in insisting angels venerate him.
It is the jealous prophesy fulfilled,

29

Then the work of pleading starts,
The self-defense . . . finally the arrogant
Rejection . . . all in the feel of injury
That comes from loving a God whose love
Cannot be limited to one alone . . . so, Satan
Is a lover—failed in love—loving only
Others' failures now. He did not fall through
Hate but through possessiveness in love.
Yet still he teaches us love's urgency, albeit
In a crooked way we have to straighten
In ourselves . . . even by our deaths.
We must surrender heaven and bear with hell.
Love is His gift of nothing but Himself
To the heart entrapped in the hell
Of empty longings and attachments. It is where
We find Him and ourselves.
Failed lovers teach—the only failure is to love.

IBN ATA

Love is no match for power
In this world.

30

HALLAJ

Power is not our domain, my friend.

IBN ATA

But if it isn't, God will not triumph
In this world. I don't believe you understand
What power is.

HALLAJ

Not as one who has ever wielded it,
So its concealments are not seen on my face,
Nor as one who has ever desired it,
So my memories are not full of its pains.
But perhaps I am to be its victim, so
I see it as one it desires to destroy.
I am myself quite powerless and see
Power only in friendship, in moments
Of humor shared, of unsolicited
Generosity, of love . . . in God's

31

Predisposition for irrelevance,
Which is a careless foretaste of Himself.
Power is an exercise in controlled frustration
That God's and your opinions differ,
In which the tongue and heart are inharmonious.
How hard it is to strive for harmony,
How powerless we are.

IBN ATA

But power can be exercised for good.
I think it is better to attempt it
Than to be too easily accepting.

HALLAJ

Unfortunately I am a failure at that, too.
Perhaps I thought the best of everyone,
More likely I just never formed a stance
On what men were or how I should behave
And calling me "naive," removing me

32

From worldliness, as teachers did, was just
The start of judging me unfit to live.
I am. It's true. All circles I was in
Bisected one another and the Truth came out.
Do not follow my imprudences, please
My friend, only the Truth that speaks to you.
I know I must detach you from my sins.
I know I must not keep you to myself.
The most terrible possession is the old
Man's grasp upon the young who thinks him wise.
I love your coming back to hear a fool.

IBN ATA

How could this happen?
How could God let the scoundrels rule the world?
The world and the heavens are His, we know
From His eternal Word. A brilliant jurist
Who is jealous, a corrupt vizir
And a slothful caliph, conspire to end
Your teaching and (*he says softly*) your life.
How do you explain their seeming triumph?

HALLAJ

By your word *seeming*. Scoundrels have small goals
For which their lives have set high stakes. My death
Is not momentous as a goal to me
But their continued need for power
Depends on it. Their triumph
May not last too long. It may appear
Much less important when I'm dead.
But scoundrels never think ahead. Longevity
Is useless, for they must work fast.
But there is always someone played upon
And one who plays—a scoundrel is two men,
Thus neither thinks he's bad within himself:
Just as a saint is two, two friends
Whom God transforms to one through love. No one
Is saint alone, only self-righteous. The friends
Of God have much to learn from scoundrels,
Who know that nothing can be gained
From solitude. . . . But I do not want
To spend my final hours on scoundrels
And their dupes, but rather on the things that

34

Must and will survive, for always
We begin again in a world
That is the same, His world. We rebuild
Anew what is torn down, we bury in
New ground a seed from what
Has lived in Truth and water it
As serving maids. In seven days
A plant will grow. We always must
Renew ~~renew renew~~ . . . as knows our One creative Truth,
The Merciful and the Compassionate;
That's what I want my life and death to mean.

IBN ATA

The wicked triumph through our decadence
And our addiction to images, which God condemns.

HALLAJ

The wicked may triumph.
Our decadence will take care of itself.

35

IBN ATA

How can you still dismiss with glibness
What God condemns?

HALLAJ

If I had been a different kind of man
Or God had used me in another way,
I would have been upset at others'
Images and decadence and all that our
Civilization parades about of vacant beauty,
But the only image I detest is
What grows from myself, the sight itself
Of my own being, always imagining roles
God gives me to play before the substance
Has been given me by Him to play them,
Always anticipating and wasting God, until I have
To wear disguises to hide me to myself.
Our attachment to our uncreated self
We're striving to create above all else
To show the world—that is idolatry.

36

That is why we're failed lovers and abuse
His angels whom He sends to rescue us
By asking us for hospitality
In our ruined cities. Our failure
To achieve the glory we imagine
For ourselves leaves only its dead odor.
Now He has given me the chance to break
The image I have faced. The idol of myself. . . .

IBN ATA

I can't accept what you are saying now.
Those whom He loves He does not treat this way.
Is the heart merely a plaything of God?
No, I see, you are teasing me again.

HALLAJ

No, I am not teasing. But you begin
To perceive me, though you mustn't follow me.
You know, my friend, our surgeons prove to us
That our hearts have two chambers that contain

37

A mixture of blood and of living breath.
They are analogous to the spirit and reason,
To divine inspiration and human expiration.
He gives us consciousness within our heart,
And *we* become with Him the One Who gives us life.
I was a corpse He reclothed as a body.
We each are His epiphanies, we see
In each of us the presence He has made;
The action He has given us, the life.
His whole creation is aglow with life.
And we respond to it through what's alive
In us. I was in ecstasy last night
Embracing and embraced by Him, as one
Small residue of life. When I am gone
I know He'll breathe into my heart again.

    (Pauses)

Let us rest from words.

    IBN ATA

No, master, I cannot let you stop.
There isn't time.

38

HALLAJ

Yes, I know;
Time becomes precious at a certain age.
We lose our sense of being wholly lost
Only to find our next dilemma, time.
We see but have too little time to change.
The world we seek is all too evident.
We even have the power of words and faith
To make it almost be. Our Truth is there,
Hovering to take us out of time.
And now, when time's irrelevant at last,
We need it as we languish here in jail
Between the visits of our sons and friends.
We have too little time alone with them.
We know the way to read the hearts we love.
Like branches that have lost their leaves,
Captive in the cold we cry for clothes
Paraded in our old humiliation
On the esplanade. The wind grieves loud for us
As we stand numb, the stranger no one knows.
I have looked through hearts,
Through tiny vein-like branches into skies

39

With only face-like vapors passing through.
Do you think I'm mad?

IBN ATA

You are not afraid of death.
That is strange. Perhaps you are.
I think I am afraid of you.

HALLAJ

That is why He maddens us to death,
To free the others of their fear of it,
Through love of the mad one who must die.
We do not really die when we are desperate . . .
When we are carried beyond loss . . .
Beyond grief.
We do not go mad or die, we dance . . .
We dance we dance we dance. . . .

HAMD NARRATING

My father danced alone. Ibn Ata stared,
Frightened at first. He then was drawn to his feet

40

And followed him around the cell, until
He too had entered his master's dance,
Beyond his fear, beyond his sense of coming loss.
Each danced in union, without words.

*   *   *

Part Two

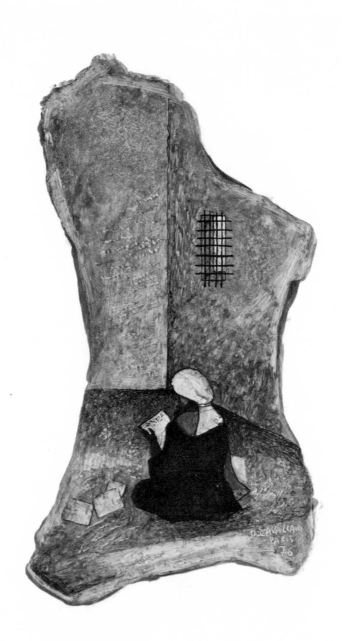

HAMD NARRATING

There were those who shadowed my father and
His disciple, keeping surveillance on
Their friendship. The one who was most disturbed
By them, whom some called jealous and whose views
Were deeply felt, was Ibn Dawud.

*   *   *

IBN DAWUD

I've always hated zealots like these two friends.
True masters say we must arrange our lives
In order and with self-restraint and grace,
Each aspect separate and well-defined,
So that one's heart and mind are not confused

45

With one another as to aims and understandings.
Each love has its domain: concupiscence
And procreation here, community cooperation
There; friendship between men here, the adoration
Of transcendence there. Only God can unify.
How reckless Hallaj is. He is
Attached to God as to his friends. He mixes
Everything together in a way
Destined to destroy him. We shall see him
Die for his presumption. For only God
Knows how to embrace the truth; not in
The Christian way, but without passion,
In pure detachment beyond even Himself.
And we must imitate His quieter creation,
As a bouquet is arranged,
To enhance its beauty, or a room
In which one lives in measured taste.
Truth is an idea and an attribute
Of God. Hallaj ignores such distinctions.
He knows directly, so he claims, the mind
Of God, but he ignores the fact
That others are incapable of following

His way. We may not have his courage,
Yet he goes on and makes us feel afraid.
That is an inward sign to me that he is wrong.
I know he's not a charlatan, as some may say,
But he is dangerous, and so must die.

2

HAMD NARRATING

Ibn Dawud questioned Ibn Ata,
Trying one final time to dissuade him
From adhering to my father's teaching
And to endorse the legal condemnation.

*   *   *

IBN ATA

He would agree with that.

47

IBN DAWUD

That we are illusions, of course . . . but would
He agree that our minds must be preoccupied
With distinguishing illusion from reality,
Not with illusory unions with God?
No, there you are silent, interpreter.

IBN ATA

He would say, God is the distinguisher,
We the dwellers in the cave; the seven
Sleepers trusted, they did not insist
The meaning be immediately clear.

IBN DAWUD

How far would you follow your master in
Such simplicity?

IBN ATA

I would follow him anywhere.
He is not filled with illusion.
He is totally real.

48

IBN DAWUD

But your simplicity is not as old
And wise as his. It will too soon expose
You to a disciple's fate.
You should be afraid of him, my friend;
Aren't you?

IBN ATA

No.

IBN DAWUD

Then what makes you persist in interpreting
His madness in a favorable light?
Are you ready to join him on the gibbet?

IBN ATA

What are you saying?

49

IBN DAWUD

I am saying that one who supports him
As indiscriminately as you do
May have to share the legal consequence.

IBN ATA

Is that a threat?
What legal consequence?

IBN DAWUD

I did not mean to alarm you.
I understand your hesitation now.
You did not know the implications of
Your friendship for him. Words can be seductive,
Leading one, without one's knowing, to share
The fate of one's seducer: death,
In this instance, for promulgating
Unsound notions of the mind of God
And man's approach to it;

50

And for thereby undermining public order.
The penalties are clear. If you draw back
Now, you need not be involved. Understand?
Everything we say and do affects
The order of our lives. Controls exist
To reaffirm our self-controls. He's broken them
And must be broken in their name. I think
The point is clear. You seem to grasp it now.
Your face is calm. Prudence is the proper
Management of fear. I wish we met in
Other ways, for you are sensitive. I
See what you must mean to him. It is too bad.

IBN ATA

I do not need your sympathy just now.
I see I also was not called to prudence.

IBN DAWUD

I have tried to talk sense to you, but you
Persist. Now you make me angry.

51

The witnesses have signed the condemnation.
Only you refuse, though you are a legal
Witness to his crime.

IBN ATA

I am a witness, accredited like
All the rest, just as you say, but unlike them
Not to his crime. He is a friend of God
And of yourself, myself, and all of these.
He preached the truth.

IBN DAWUD

He broke the law. You know his teaching on
The pilgrimage—

IBN ATA

It's sound. He aims it at
The spirit of the law: *(reads)*
"When a man wants to carry out the pilgrimage

52

And has no way of doing it,
He must set aside a room in his own house
Which no one enters, where no one goes,
And which no one may pass through.
Then, at the time of pilgrimage
He must walk around it seven times,
And perform the other rituals, as at Mecca.
When this is done, he will gather thirty orphans,
Prepare for them the finest of meals
In this special room, serve them himself,
Wash them and dress them in new clothes,
And give them each seven drachmas.
All this will satisfy the hajj for him."

     IBN DAWUD

He undermines Islam itself.
The Prophet taught sobriety and patience.

     IBN ATA

He taught the spirit of the pilgrimage,
As Hallaj does,

53

Against idolaters of stones and gold
The pilgrims spend. We've grown idolatrous
In the Prophet's name. Hallaj awakens us
As the Prophet once did.

IBN DAWUD

Now you have blasphemed!
You must retract to save your life.
The Prophet never claimed that he was God.

IBN ATA

Hallaj said only "the Truth has entered
Me, I am the Truth, no longer I myself. . . ."
What heresy can experts find in that?

IBN DAWUD

God never told us He could enter us.
Do you believe in union like your friend?

IBN ATA

The way to union is fraternal love.

IBN DAWUD

God could not love such fools as you or he!
You persist in this insane position!

IBN ATA

As you do in your jealous coldness!
Which is no better than our base vizir's
Hoarding of the people's grain and gold.

IBN DAWUD

I have no further time to waste on you.
I give you both to Hamid's province now.

55

3

HAMD NARRATING

Ibn Ata saw my father again.
The disciple's face was ashen
And his life seemed drained.
It was their final visit together.

*   *   *

HALLAJ

Immersion is what God requires of us,
Not prudence or restraint. He is the sea
And signals us to lose ourselves in Him.
We are poor swimmers and the undertow
Is frightening, but the water's edge
Attracts us breathless. We go to the sea

56

To draw its steady breathing, like the
Camel at the well, to replenish ourselves.
We must conquer our fear, we must plunge much
Deeper, for God is deeper than water.

IBN ATA

But are you ready for death?
Aren't you afraid at all?

HALLAJ

Of course, I am a person like yourself.
I am afraid. But prayer distracts me
By His words, which are my faithful friends,
And He has given me a special grace:
My consciousness of time is very poor.
All of my life I have been late and now
At last I realize why: I do not know
How close is death, how little time I have.
Some know this too precisely, I believe,
And are impatient with the time they have

57

Or time they think that others waste for them.
No time is wasted, really, and no love.
Now talking on too long has a purpose . . .
To distract myself from fear. . . .
I see my jailor. I must let you go.

IBN ATA

Will I see you again, master?

HALLAJ

Yes, when I am on the esplanade.
We may not have a chance to speak,
But don't be afraid nor try to join me.
For your way is yours, don't imitate mine.
You'll find your way.

IBN ATA

When, master?

58

HALLAJ

When in a crowd or alone you perceive
Impatience disappearing, and you know
Just where you are and where
You're meant to be.

IBN ATA

Where is that, master?

HALLAJ

Anywhere. You will know your action.
You are present there, not thinking of some-
Where else you ought to be.

IBN ATA

I am afraid without you, master,
Not hearing your words.
Can you bequeath me a maxim
To hold and live by in your absence?

59

HALLAJ

Only to subdue yourself or yourself
Will subdue you. I am not afraid for you,
And don't be afraid of being labelled strange.
There is a freedom in strangeness.
Exposure frees us from anxiety.
You must leave now.
The jailor is upset by long farewells.

HAMD NARRATING

Ibn Ata seized his hand and buried his face
In it, then rose with tears in his eyes,
And ran out of the cell.

HALLAJ

I am afraid we shall not meet again.
I see my own death nearer in his leaving me.

*　　*　　*

60

Part Three

1

(After a long silence Hallaj speaks:)

We are here, we, Your witnesses.
We ask for refuge in the splendor of Your Glory
That You may show at last what You intended
To fashion and achieve,
O You Who are God in heaven and on earth.

It is You Who shine forth when You desire
Just as You shone before the angels and Satan
In the most beautiful form of the unspoiled Adam,
The form in which Your voice resides
Present in knowledge and in speech.

You have given me, Your present witness,
Your self, Your own desire. . . .
How is it that You Who gave me Your Self
When they had stripped and mocked me for my self,

63

Who used me to proclaim Your Self,
To utter the words which gave me life,
Have let me be taken, imprisoned, judged,
Now to be executed, hung on the cross,
Burned, my ashes to be thrown to the winds
Of the desert, the waves of the Tigris. . . .
Am I of no use once Your words are spoken . . . ?
Should I have not revealed Your gift of Your Self
As my enemies say who love the vanity
Of possessing You alone? Do you abandon me
Or can the smallest particle of my ashes
Burned in this way to Your glory
Assure me of another form in Your love
Than this old temple they are tearing down?

        *   *   *

HAMD NARRATING

Ibn Ata was put to death by Hamid
For starting a demonstration on

My father's behalf. Indeed, it was said
His demonstration made my father's fate
Much worse, for Hamid's anger was increased
By it. I knew Ibn Ata had lost
His self-composure and perhaps his sense,
For in a moment of desperation
In which he hurt me he said "You have not
Been as true a son to your father as
I have." He was very close to him as
A disciple, and did not mean the things
He said. My father shared his heart with him.

The one who had supported him for years,
Who kept him from imprisonment at first
By intervening with her son, but lost
The struggle when Hamid became vizir,
Was Shaghab, the mother of the Caliph,
Who loved my father and who came to see
Him in his cell the night before his death.

2

SHAGHAB

Ibn Ata has been put to death.
Hamid knew my son would bow to him
When the thought of hearing a long story
Became too bothersome. Hamid knows
How to condense long tales.

HALLAJ

I know.
Our friendships now are foretastes of heaven.

SHAGHAB

What do you mean by foretastes. You speak in
Riddles.

66

HALLAJ

Not at all. I've never liked such things as
Riddles, plays on words, or anything obscure.
I am inclined to love, not to prove brightness.
Foretastes are precious moments that we live
With one another as one lives with God
In intimate relaxation through His gesture.

SHAGHAB

Do you remember them when you're alone
In your cell without visitors or guards.

HALLAJ

No, for I'm afraid of living too enclosed
In moments that are past. A foretaste
Is of things to come. A guard's shared humor,
The glint of horror in a hangman's face, death itself
I want to be awake to. I ask that

Nothing be held back. Executioners have fatigues.
We are one humanity.

SHAGHAB

But somehow
You have managed to escape the merely
Reasonable
That keeps most men inured to truth.
What is your secret, how have you achieved
The luxury of only seeming mad?

HALLAJ

Perhaps it is no luxury. Perhaps I am.

SHAGHAB

I knew You'd say that. With you I dread
My own addiction to the obvious.
We are all bored at what we say, not just
My son or his commensals, but all
Of us confined by our triumph and richness

In the world. We luxuriate in power
While underneath a constant drain
Of mental energy depletes us. Our thoughts
Are dead or add to death. That is our fate.
Yet somehow you escaped. I don't ask how
But only to be allowed to say the
Obvious to you, for unlike all of us
You do not seem afraid of it. Have you
Ever been bored?

HALLAJ

When I was very young,
Before I left my birthplace of Bayda
I was truly bored, I don't remember why,
But I remember the experience
Of idleness, of wanting to be somewhere else,
Feeling time to be in endless supply.

SHAGHAB

I would like to remember boredom, not
Endure it. Tell me how?

69

HALLAJ

By surrendering the self, by releasing
Prize possessions from their cages—
One's song, one's taste, one's sense of beauty . . .
That ties one to oneself.

SHAGHAB

But you are tied.

HALLAJ

I shall be released before long.

SHAGHAB

In my boredom I have imagined pain
As something beautiful, sorrow as heart-
Filling music. I even dreamed
I saw you crucified, your arms were wings
And you took flight in soaring ecstasy

70

To God, you flew with other creatures
In your folds. Suffering seemed bliss.

    HALLAJ

I differ with your dream on that.

    SHAGHAB

No, suffering cannot be given you
Except to veil your flight.

    HALLAJ

That is the precious singing bird you cage
But will release in time. . . .

    SHAGHAB

I am a very poor disciple, but I think
I see behind your veils and disguises,
Your talk about your love of pleasure, your

71

Words that bring you close to men, for I
Am able to distinguish those
Who are captive to our world from those
Who are merely clothed in it. You have no
Attachments, you live an asceticism
Of the heart. For you your final suffering
Will bring you joy, but it will bring us
Pain of loss. That is why I woke up
Crying in my dream. I understand
You though I am a caliph's mother.
You hold the secret truth we can't embrace.
And you must appear in this or that
Disguise, for you are the first of our faith
Who desires to die out of sheer love.
You are very frightening to some and
Even to me. I know the way it will end.

HALLAJ

You understand our God is a consuming fire.
The rose opens to the light, the Narcissus
Leans to shade. We are more mixtures than we

72

Like to think. But at some point His light
Penetrates our eyes, destroying our shades
And our distortions, leaving us floating blind
Spots we forget when our vision is clarified in His.
If we are roses we are drawn to light.
We do not think about the end. There is none.

SHAGHAB

May I ask you something very personal?

HALLAJ

I have nothing personal that is my own.

SHAGHAB

I have a very small idea of love:
That it requires two at once, and it lives
On two occurrences: intimacy and laughter.
We must enjoy the presence of the one we love
And find amusement in the world we share.

Have you known that with others or with God
Alone?

HALLAJ

(He smiles.) With both, not God alone.

> *(She smiles and reaches out to touch his hands.*
> *They break together in releasing laughter.)*

HAMD NARRATING

I came to the prison to see and talk
With my father for the last time.
When I entered, we embraced.

74

HAMD

Father.

HALLAJ

Let me withdraw alone.
You know I am with you.

> *(Hamd sits down on a bench in one corner of the cell.
> Hallaj stands alone across the cell for a time.)*

HALLAJ

I cry to You, not only for myself
But for those souls who yearn for You,
Whose witness, I myself, goes now to you,
The witness of Eternity.

*   *   *

HAMD NARRATING

He stood silent for several minutes, I
Remember, then he cried out "illusion!"
And wept. Hours later I heard my father
Huddled in his mantle whisper:
"Can no one free me from God?"

4

HAMD NARRATING

On the morning of the execution
He was taken from his prison,
Put on one of the pack mules,
Led away, jostled by grooms
Who ran alongside him
Shouting at the crowd which formed

76

A mob. The commissioner,
Afraid himself of being killed
Or of someone killing his prisoner,
Said: "This is not Hallaj,
Hallaj is in the Palace of Vizirs."
While Hamid's mounted guard
Escorted him, the commissioner,
To the esplanade, near the Khurasani
Gate, on the West Bank of the Tigris
Where the gibbet was set up.
Everyone who lived in Baghdad
And hundreds of foreign visitors
To the City of Peace were there.
Never had such a crowd formed
To witness an execution.
The guards lifted him from the mule
And he began dancing in his chains.
The guards were shocked, the people
Who could see burst into nervous laughter,
And then they led him to the gibbet.
They tore the clothes from his back
And began the ordered flagellation.

77

"Now Constantinople is taken!" he shouted,
At the five hundredth lash. He fainted
And the commissioner ordered
The flagellation stopped
Lest he die without suffering
The full prescribed punishment.
The guards had been ordered to close their ears
Lest they be seduced to show him mercy.
Once the lashes had been stopped
The executioner cut off one of his hands
And then a foot, and then the other hand
Followed as prescribed by the other foot.
He then was hoisted on the gibbet in display.
The air was filled with screams.
The commissioner ordered the decapitation
Postponed until the morning
So the vizir, Hamid, could be present.
That night his friends and enemies
Came to him, challenging him
To answer for himself. Looters
Roamed the city, setting fire to shops.
Baghdad was convulsed with rioting.
He cried out to God: "O my Friend, my Friend. . . . "

His disciples came . . . and said
To the gibbet: "Have we not forbidden you
To receive a guest, neither angel nor man!"
One threw a rose at my father,
Who raised his bloody stump
And wiped his cheek
Where it had struck him.
Life ebbed from him
And he could barely speak.
In the morning Hamid came.
He had ordered the official witnesses
At the trial scattered through the crowd
To cry out: "This is for the salvation
Of Islam. Let his blood fall on our necks!"
Advancing toward the gibbet Hamid drew
From his sleeve a scroll which he handed
To the commissioner to unroll.
The latter handed it back to him. It had
The names of eighty-four learned men on it,
The legal scholars and Koran reciters,
Attesting to his heresy. A placard
Was raised that later would be pinned
To his head, saying "this is the head

Of the blasphemous conniver and deceiver
Husayn Ibn Mansur al-Hallaj,
One whom God has put to death
At the hands of Caliph al-Muqtadir
After proof was given showing that he claimed
The sovereignty of God himself.
Glory be to God, Who causes his blood
To be shed and led him to be cursed."
The crowd shouted: God is great!
Hamid then called for the witnesses
To reenact the trial, as was prescribed,
Arguing the pros and cons and finally
Concurring with the statement read.
Hamid then asked: "The Caliph is innocent
Of his blood?" They shouted "Yes!"
"The commissioner is innocent of his blood?"
"Yes. Let his blood fall on our necks!"
Then Hamid returned the scroll to his sleeve
And lowered his right hand. The executioner
Stepped forward and the guards took
My father down. As he was being lowered
He cried out "the ecstatic
Wants only to be alone with his Only One."

The executioner beheaded him.
His body was wrapped in his mantle
And doused with oil and set aflame
Together with his books
The sellers had been ordered to bring forth.
One half-crazed disciple came forward
And pushed at the coals with his stick,
Saying to them "Speak!"
Some said "Like Jesus he could not die.
Another took his place."
And others said he stole the word God gave him
To keep in secret and used it to exalt himself.
And that is why he was put to death.
The ashes were taken up and thrown
From a minaret into the Tigris.
His head was carried to the Caliph's palace
Across the Tigris on the Bridge of Boats.
It was hung on a gate for everyone to see.
The walls of the palace behind him were high.
The power and majesty of what men build
Is awesome.

*   *   *